SPIDERS AROUND THE WORLD

All About North American WOLF SPIDERS

John Bankston

Mitchell Lane
PUBLISHERS

2001 SW 31st Avenue
Hallandale, FL 33009
www.mitchelllanepub.com

Little Mitchie

First Edition, 2025.

Author: John Bankston
Designer: Ed Morgan
Editor: Morgan Brody

Little Mitchie is an imprint of Mitchell Lane Publishers.

Title: All About North American Wolf Spiders
Description: Hallandale, FL : Mitchell Lane Publishers, [2025]

Series: Spiders Around the World: North America
Library bound ISBN: 978-1-68020-938-9
eBook ISBN: 978-1-68020-939-6
Paperback ISBN: 979-8-89260-165-8

Photo credits: pp. 4-5, 20-21 wikimedia; balance Shutterstock

Contents

A wolf spider is on the hunt. Eight eyes cover its face. The spider sees very well. It's also fast.

The beetle is nearby. It tries to run. The spider gives chase. Then it shoots webbing over the bug. It makes a ball of beetle and silk. The spider bites. **Venom** kills the beetle. Now it's food.

Wolf spiders don’t use webs to catch **prey**. They run and hunt. They are lone wolf spiders.

Besides beetles, they also like ants and grasshoppers. Wolf spiders can be prey for other **predators**. Birds and lizards love wolf spider snacks. People also kill them.

Wolf spiders sleep all day. They hunt at night. This means they are **nocturnal**. Four of its eyes **reflect** light. They glow in the dark.

These spiders can be gray, brown, or black. They also have shades of orange or tan. This lets them blend in where they live. You can find wolf spiders in fields and in forests. They also call mountains and deserts their home. They have even been found near volcanoes. They don't mind living with people.

Female wolf spiders are over an inch long. That's bigger than your thumb! Their legs are twice as long as their bodies. Males are half the size of females. Unlucky males get killed after **mating**.

Females lay dozens of egg sacs. She keeps them on her back. She'll do the same after they hatch. She'll give her **spiderlings** piggyback rides. The wolf spider is the only spider that does this.

These spiders are hairy and scary. Their venom doesn't harm people. Just don't pick one up. Wolf spider bites hurt!

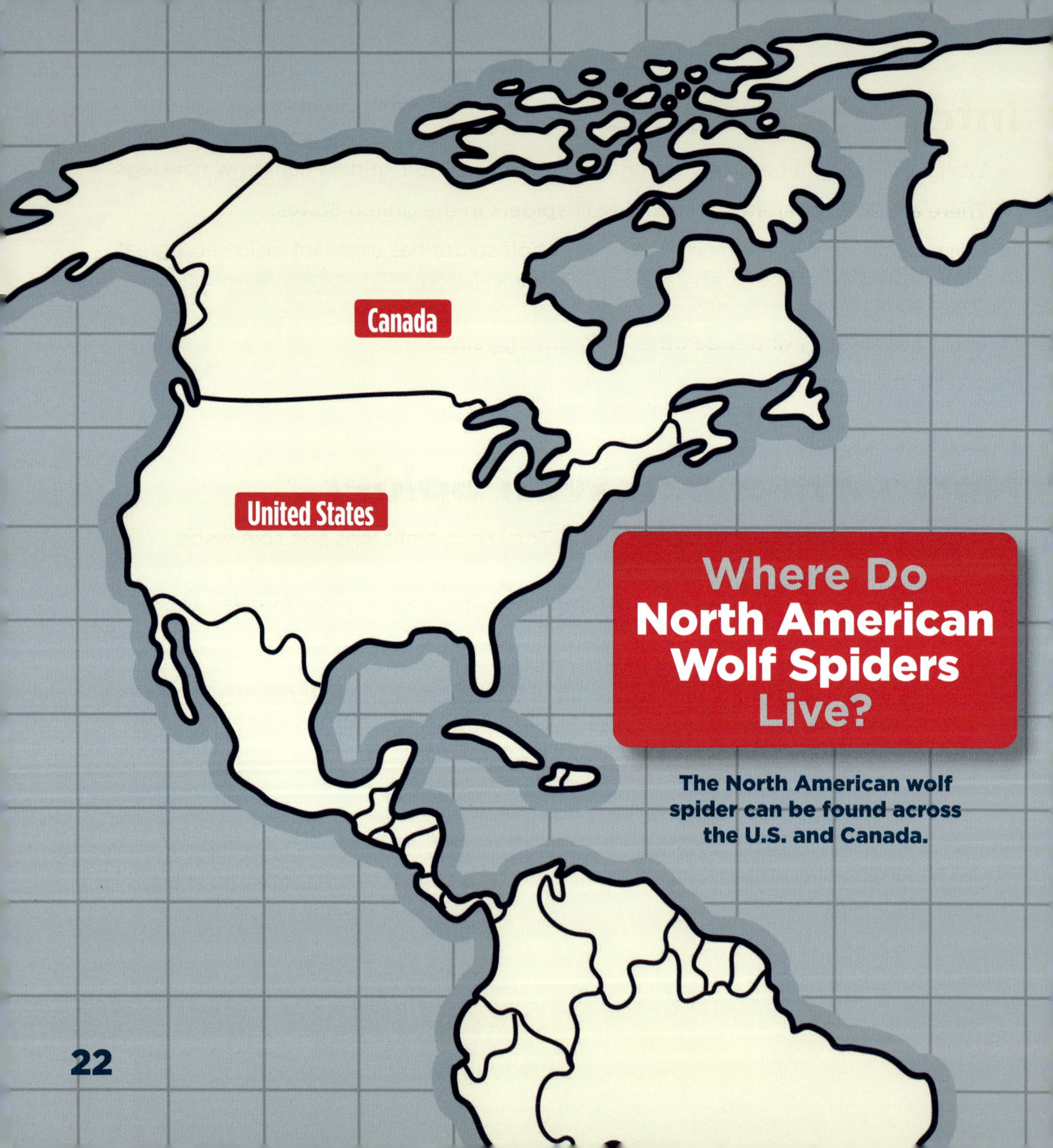

Where Do **North American Wolf Spiders** Live?

The North American wolf spider can be found across the U.S. and Canada.

Interesting Facts

- Wolf spiders will let a predator run off with its leg. Wolf spiders can grow new legs.
- There are 200 different **species** of wolf spiders in the United States.
- Most **arachnids** have poor vision but the Wolf spider has excellent vision and great running abilities. They chase down their prey but they can hold still to wait for crawling insects to get close by.
- Females will carry and raise other female's egg sacs.

Parts of a North American Wolf Spider

Spiders are not insects. They are arachnids. They have eight legs and spin webs.

Abdomen
The **abdomen** is thick and much bigger than the head. This is where females will carry egg sacs and spiderlings.

Eyes
Wolf spiders have very large eyes. There are four eyes above the mouth. It also has two eyes at the top of its head and two more at the front of its head. None of these eyes move.

Legs
Their legs have three claws at the end.

Mouth
Two long strings called **pedipalps** hang from their mouth. Males use them to attract females. They can also grab prey.

Glossary

abdomen (ab-DOE-men)
Place where the stomach is located

arachnids (a-rack-NIDS)
An eight-legged creature without antenna

mating (MAYT-ing)
When male and females of the same species come together to create offspring

nocturnal (noc-TURN-al)
Something that is most active at night

pedipalps (peda-PALP)
Long strings that look like legs and hang from the spider's mouth

predator (pred-a-TOR)
Animal that hunts and eats other animals for food

prey (pray)
Animal hunted by another for food

reflect ree-FLEK)
Shooting back light

species (spee-CEES)
Similar animals that can have offspring

spiderlings (spider-er-LING)
A baby spider

Further Reading

All Things Spiders For Kids: Filled With Plenty of Facts, Photos, and Fun to Learn all About Spiders. Berlin, Germany: Admore Publishing, 2022.

Archer, Claire. *Wolf Spiders*. Minneapolis, MN: Abdo Kids, 2015.

On the Internet

Discover some interesting facts about the North American Wolf spider from A-to-Z Animals:
https://a-z-animals.com/animals/wolf-spider/

Learn all about them from Biokids at the University of Michigan:
http://www.biokids.umich.edu/critters/Lycosidae/

See more from the Missouri Department of Conservation:
https://mdc.mo.gov/discover-nature/field-guide/wolf-spiders

Index